ALSO BY KENNETH KOCH

POETRY

Sun Out   2002
A Possible World   2002
New Addresses   2000
Straits   1998
One Train   1994
On the Great Atlantic Rainway, Selected Poems 1950–1988   1994
Seasons on Earth   1987
On the Edge   1986
Selected Poems: 1950–1982   1985
Days and Nights   1982
The Burning Mystery of Anna in 1951   1979
The Duplications   1977
The Art of Love   1975
The Pleasures of Peace   1969
When the Sun Tries to Go On   1969
Thank You and Other Poems   1962
Permanently   1961
Ko, or A Season on Earth   1960

FICTION

Hotel Lambosa   1993
The Red Robins   1975

THEATER

The Gold Standard: A Book of Plays   1996
One Thousand Avant-Garde Plays   1988
The Red Robins   1979
A Change of Hearts   1973
Bertha and Other Plays   1966

NONFICTION

A Possible World

A Possible World

POEMS

Kenneth Koch

ALFRED A. KNOPF   NEW YORK   2002

THIS IS A BORZOI BOOK
PUBLISHED BY ALFRED A. KNOPF

Some of the poems in this collection have been previously published,
some of them in slightly different form, in the following:
American Poetry Review: "Roma non basta una vita"
The American Scholar: "On the Acropolis"
Boulevard: "At Extremes," "Variations at Home and Abroad"
Fence: "Possible World"
The New Yorker: "A Big Clown-Face-Shaped Cloud," "Mountain," "Paradiso"
New York Review of Books: "Proverb," "Zones"
Poetry: "Bel Canto," "A Momentary Longing to Hear Sad Advice from One Long Dead"
Raritan: "Flight"
Visionaire: "Expansive Water"

Library of Congress Cataloging-in-Publication Data

Koch, Kenneth, 1995–2002.
A possible world : poems / Kenneth Koch.—1st ed.
p.   cm.
ISBN 0-375-41492-4
I. Title.

PS3521.O27 P67 2002
811'.54—dc21
20022072477

Manufactured in the United States of America
First Edition

TO KAREN

Contents

.

A Possible World

Bel Canto

The sun is high, the seaside air is sharp,
And salty light reveals the Mayan School.
The Irish hope their names are on the harp,
We see the sheep's advertisement for wool,
Boulders are here, to throw against a tarp,
From which comes bursting forth a puzzled mule.
Perceval seizes it and mounts it, then
The blood-dimmed tide recedes and then comes in again.

Fateful connections that we make to things
Whose functioning's oblivious to our lives!
How sidewise news of light from darkness springs,
How blue bees buzz from big blooms back to hives
And make the honey while the queen bee sings
Leadbelly in arrangements by Burl Ives—
How long ago I saw the misted pine trees
And hoped, no matter how, to get them into poetry!

Stendhal, at fifty, gazing, as it happened,
On Rome from the Janiculum, decided
That one way he could give his life a stipend
Was to suspend his being Amour's fighter
And get to know himself. Here he had ripened,
Accomplished, loved, and lived, was a great writer
But never had explored in true detail
His childhood and his growing up. So he set sail

Composing *La Vie de Henry Brulard*
But in five hundred pages scarcely got
Beyond his seventeenth year, for it is hard
To take into account what happens here
And fit it all onto an index card.
Even one moment of it is too hot,
Complex and cannibalistically connected
To every other, which is what might be expected.

Sterne's hero has a greater problem, never
Getting much past his birth. I've had a third one.
My autobiography, if I should ever
Start out to write it, quickly seems a burden,
An I-will-do-that-the-next-time endeavor.
Whatever life I do write's an absurd one
As if some crazy person with a knife
Cut up and made a jigsaw puzzle of a life.

In any case a life that's hardly possible
In the conditions that we really live in,
Where easy flying leaps to inaccessible
Mountainy places where love is a given
And misery, if there, infinitesimal,
Are quite the norm. Here none by pain is driven
That is not curable by the romanza
That's kept in readiness to finish any stanza.

Whatever, then, I see at this late stage of
My life I may or may not have stayed ignorant
Of that great book I've strained to write one page of
Yet always hoping my page was significant.
Be it or not, for me and for the ages,
I leave it as it is. Yet as a figurant
Who has not stopped, I'm writing in addition
More lines to clarify my present disposition.

One person in a million finds out something
Perhaps each fifty years and that is knowledge.
Newton, Copernicus, Einstein are cunning;
The rest of us just rise and go to college
With no more hope to come home with the bunting
Than a stray dachshund going through the village.
However, what a treat our small successes
Of present and of past, at various addresses!

To be in all those places where I tarried
Too little or too late or bright and early,
To love again the first woman I married,
To marvel at such things as melancholy,
Sophistication, drums, a baby carriage,
A John Cage concert heard at Alice Tully—
How my desire, when young to be a poet
Made me attentive and oblivious every moment!

Do you remember Oceanview the Fair?
The heights above the river? The canoes?
The place we beached them and the grass was bare?
Those days the sand bars gave our knees a truce?
The crooked line of pantry shelves, with pear
And cherry jam? And Pancho, with his noose?
Do you remember Full and Half and Empty?
Do you remember sorrow standing in the entry?

Do you remember thought, and talking plainly?
Michel and I went walking after Chartres
Cathedral had engaged our spirits mainly
By giving us an insight into Barthes.
Michel said he was capable of feigning
Renewed intentions of the soul's deep part,
Like this cathedral's artificial forces
That press a kind of artless thought into our faces.

And yet—The moor is dark beneath the moon.
The porcupine turns over on its belly
And new conceptions rap at the cocoon.
Civilization, dealing with us fairly,
For once, releases its Erechtheum
Of understanding, which consoles us, nearly.
Later we study certain characteristics
That may give us a better chance with the statistics.

How much I'd like to live the whole thing over,
But making some corrections as I go!
To be a better husband and a father,
Be with my babies on a sled in snow.
By twenty I'd have understood my mother
And by compassion found a way to know
What separates the what-I-started-out-as
From what-I sometimes-wished-I-was-when-in-the-mountains.

To be once more the one who what was worthy
Of courtship courted—it was quite as stressful
As trying to, er, as they say, give birth to
A poem and as often unsuccessful,
But it was nice to be sublime and flirty
With radiant girls, and, in some strange way, restful.
I could be everything I wasn't usually—
And then to get somebody else to feel it mutually!

In poems the same problem or a similar.
Desire of course not only to do old things
But things unheard of yet by nuns or visitors
And of the melancholy finch be co-finch
In singing songs with such a broad parameter
That seamstresses would stare, forget to sew things,
Astronauts quit the sky, athletes the stadium
To hear them, and the rest of what they hear be tedium.

Such wild desires, I think it's recognizable
Are part and parcel of the Human Image
And in a way, I'd say, no less predictable
Than Popeye's feelings for a can of spinach.
Yet if we're set on course by the Invisible,
All predetermined, what about the language
That teases me each morning with its leanings
Toward the Unprogrammed Altitudes beyond its meanings?

Are you, O particles, O atoms, nominatives
Like Percevals and Stendhals, set in motion
By some Ordaining Will that is definitive?
Is this invading chill and high emotion,
This tendency to know one is regenerative,
Is this, all, tidal take-home like the ocean?
Be what you may, my thanks for your society
Through the long life I've had, your jokes and your variety,

The warmth you've shown in giving me a temperature
That I can live with, and the strength you've shared with me
In arms and legs—and for your part in literature,
What can I say? It is as if life stared at me
And kissed my lips and left it as a signature.
Thank you for that, and thank you for preparing me
For love itself, and friendship its co-agent.
Thank you for being this, and for its inspiration.

A Review

Pure finality of bedding—
Intellectual life—
This article to reassure me—
Others are alive—
Then unexpectedly awake
Middle of the night—
What are they thinking—
Afraid? Probably. Succeeding
At something? Likely—
All night
Breathing, rain.

A Momentary Longing
to Hear Sad Advice from One Long Dead

Who was my teacher at Harvard. Did not wear overcoat
Saying to me we walked across the Yard
Cold brittle autumn is you should be wearing overcoat. I said
You are not wearing overcoat. He said
You should do as I say not do as I do.
Just how American it was and how late Forties it was
Delmore, but not I, was probably aware. He quoted *Finnegans Wake* to me
In his New York apartment sitting on chair
Table directly in front of him. There did he write? I am wondering.
Look at this photograph said of his mother and father.
Coney Island. Do they look happy? He couldn't figure it out.
Believed *Pogo* to be at the limits of our culture.
Pogo. Walt Kelly must have read Joyce Delmore said.
Why don't you ask him?
Why don't you ask Walt Kelly if he read *Finnegans Wake* or not.
Your parents don't look happy but it is just a photograph.
Maybe they felt awkward posing for photographs.
Maybe it is just a bad photograph. Delmore is not listening
I want to hear him tell me something sad but however true.
Delmore in his tomb is sitting. People say yes everyone is dying
But here read this happy book on the subject. Not Delmore. Not that
    rueful man.

Mountain

Nothing's moving I don't see anybody
And I know that it's not a trick
There really is nothing moving there
And there aren't any people. It is the very utmost top
Where, as is not unusual,
There is snow, lying like the hair on a white-haired person's head
Combed sideways and backward and forward to cover as much of the top
As possible, for the snow is thinning, it's September
Although a few months from now there will be a new crop
Probably, though this no one KNOWS (so neither do we)
But every other year it has happened by November
Except for one year that's known about, nineteen twenty-three
When the top was more and more uncovered until December fifteenth
When finally it snowed and snowed
I love seeing this mountain like a mouse
Attached to the tail of another mouse, and to another and to another
In total mountain silence
There is no way to get up there, and no means to stay.
It is uninhabitable. No roads and no possibility
Of roads. You don't have a history
Do you, mountain top? This doesn't make you either a mystery
Or a dull person and you're certainly not a truck stop.
No industry can exploit you
No developer can divide you into estates or lots
No dazzling disquieting woman can tie your heart in knots.
I could never lead my life on one of those spots
You leave uncovered up there. No way to be there
But I'm moved.

To Buddhism

How calmly and gently you approach me in Thailand
And propose that we sit down and talk
In the pollution and in the heat, that we find a little fresh air, shade, and
    talk. You
Explain some principles—I already know a few of them
From my college days when I subscribed to a periodical named *Cat's Yawn*.
    A Zen periodical,
It was so named the editor said because those words make no sense. I didn't
Understand why he said they made no sense. However, I was drawn to the
    koans.
You tell me about the two different vehicles
And the life of Gautama, which I know. You show me statues. Of which
The golden Sleeping Buddha is the most celebrated, though I find more
    moving
The riverside cliff statue carved in Bingling Si (in China)
Amazing! But where would I fit into you or you into me? It won't happen.
Reluctantly, I lose you, never having had you. This is so much in line
With what *Cat's Yawn* said about you and with what you told me
That I imagine its making you smile.

A Schoolroom in Haiti

In Haiti, Port-au-Prince, a man walked up and down the school hallways
    carrying a bull whip.
Oh, he never uses it, the school administrator said. Its purpose is only to
    instill good discipline in the students.
They were from fourteen to seventeen years old,
Boys in white shirts and white short pants. They stood up
And wouldn't sit down till the Minister of Education
Beckoned to them to do so.
They concentrated very hard on the ideas they were being given for writing
    poems.
After the officials left, they started writing their poems in Creole.
After four or five days they were asking to come forward and sing to the
    rest of the class these Creole poems. They did so.
This experiment was never repeated. The government became even more
    repressive.
One poem begins "B is for black, Bettina, a negress whom I dote on."
The assignment was a poem about the colors of the vowels or the
    consonants in the manner of Rimbaud.
What has happened to those poems? What has become of those students?
I have the poems in New York. In Haiti I had asked to teach ten-year-olds
    but I had been told
They won't be able to write well enough. The reason was they didn't know
    French,
Not well enough to be able to write poetry. Their native language was
    Creole,
The language they spoke at home, but at the Lycée Toussaint L'Ouverture
And every other school, the instruction was in French.
They were stuck behind the French language. It loomed over them a wall
Blocking out everything:
Blocked mathematics, blocked science, blocked history, blocked literature
While Creole stayed back with them, cooking up poetry
But that was all. For the most part, except for a few rich boys
Who could afford to study French in the afternoons
They were left fatally behind.

The Expansive Water

Out in the middle of the ocean
The first time
How gray and strong the expanse of water looks
This is my first time on the ocean.
I don't get seasick. At least,
I don't think so. "Greek sculptures
On certain Greek vases, low-relief ones,
Like the coast near Bari, show more a sea-struck
Kind of reality than I have ever felt
In here. Out there—" But the young woman to whom I was talking
Seemed to have lost interest. "What is
Your name?" I asked. "Ellen," she said, turning away
To join her companions at the bar.

Later when I talked to Ellen she was not interested.
Then when I talked to her later than that she was interested.
Everyone else was seasick but Ellen and me.
I hope the storm lasts, I said.
This remark was not a success. Ellen didn't care for my kind of
    conversation.
What are you looking for in someone else? I said to Ellen
And she said, Give me the ring and tell me you want a baby.
Whoaaa! I said. We've just met.
The storm died down. Ellen is walking along the gangway with someone
I think I may have seen in an old movie
But it is only a much younger counterpart to such a person,
John Gilbert, but anyway he is much too good-looking
For me to have as competition. Still, "Ellen," I cried, "I'll give you a baby!"
Kenneth, she says, you exaggerate! It's a nice day
And I am in the midmost of my youth!
Hey Ellen, says "John Gilbert," and they walk on.

La Ville de Nice

O harbor for the rich and poor
O plain yet evanescent
O married man and paramour
O peacock born of pheasant

The first time that I walked through your
Streets, still to the earth a present,
Twenty years old, on tour,
Once near my ear a husky pleasant

Voice intoned "Est-ce que tu
Ne voudrais pas la joie?"
Not knowing what to do,
I went to my hotel, l'Hôtel du Roi

Saying that surprising word (la joie)
And kept on saying it until
I'd gone from Nice to Cannes
And then kept traveling on.

Topiary Couple

The trees on the left side of the garden
Had been trimmed so that their outline resembled
A man and a woman making love.
The woman was very beautiful.
The man had a hatchet in his hand
By which it could be guessed that he was George Washington.
A cherry tree grew freely at his side.
But the woman did not seem to be Martha Washington!
What would George be doing, even as a tree, with another woman?
This was the wild side of his life
When, freed from Presidential responsibilities,
He could chop down trees and make love to women as he wanted—
Great joy, at this thought, wells up in the gardener's heart.

NOT-MARTHA: Oh, a divorce between desire and reason,
             A cumulative state, like those cherries we eat
             When all's in blossom and we take
             The next day's sufferance for the mules of now.
GEORGE WASHINGTON: Not-Martha, you have hit on a pretty tape.
             Amusing to be with like a grape
             I would carve us into every shape
             If I could really wield this hatchet—

The trees on the left side of the garden
Become more than topiary this one time.
Talking to each other they found an idle thing.
That could be an ideal thing.
They went on talking far into the night
And during the next hundred days
Until finally George Washington said to not-Martha-Washington
"It's time to be again what once we were!"
But they, trees, remain fixed, no return, from branches and leaves.

Behavior in Thailand

Walking
Up to someone to be introduced
I remember
The book on Thai etiquette I read
Never point with your finger
Or your hand, only with your head
As in soccer, with head—or foot.

It's the booming of Bangkok's traffic
And the very bad air
Pollution gives this late twentieth century
A bad name. Pollution. The great thing
Is that it (pollution) is curable
No one has even started to cure it here.

This royal dwelling has many European characteristics
Its construction is fairly recent
European innovations were considered exotic in Thailand
A hundred, even fifty years ago
Such innovations for example as a functioning bathroom.
One non-European characteristic
Is the elephant's-foot umbrella stand in the hall.

The Oriental Hotel
Is a real palace
It has two hundred bathrooms
It sits by the river
And is a grand hotel
And doesn't have an elephant's-foot stand.

A huge sleeping Buddha
Lying on his side
Is made entirely of gold
Worth inestimably more to his worshippers
Than he would be on the currency exchange
He is here, instead of there.

Buddhist monks
About seventeen to twenty-two years old
Saffron-robed, they brush past passersby on the road
As if they were the money, themselves,
The world was spending
Continually helping itself to improve.

Thai women have a historical attitude
It happened therefore it will happen again
It makes one feel like a diamond-covered wren
Of platinum-glazing oxygen
To do it again
Means being in the center where one was sent
Millions (perhaps) of years ago along with men.

The hot streets say to my feet
Sit down
But the scalding bench says
You had best get back up
And keep walking
Because here on us, it's hell.
Bright clouds whiz past.

In one kind of Buddhism (Mahayana)
You get credits for good actions
And this can help you escape from life
I.e., the life cycle which is so unsatisfactory
One such action is paying for the release of a little bird
Which will be captured again at once and recaged, and its freedom sold to
    someone else
To do this costs five baht, forty cents.

Over here, across the river
Is another city!
A water-filled half
Not streets but canals—

Here, what's reflected (houses, markets, persons)
Is all—almost all—that you see.

On one hot corner
Whatever you see
Will be there again
With not the same people
And you are not the same
But the baby will be born.

On the Acropolis

It doesn't seem as though we could die up here, does it?
The Acropolis is so old that death on it seems superfluous.
So we can afford to take some chances—
Leap off the wall! Bash statues with our heads!

God smiles down at the Acropolis. It's a good church
But with the wrong idea. Then he is distracted by his children
Scattered among the chambers of the sea.

Old friends, I am thinking of you still.
You built the Acropolis but you didn't build it for me.

The Acropolis has a uniform
That no schoolboy can wear because it is invisible.
"It goes to the Periclean School!"

When I first came to Greece
I was twenty-five years old
And I've learned so little since
That the Greeks already knew!
Almost nothing!
I don't know why this is—
Mathematics, astronomy
All have remained dim to me—
I should have applied myself!
My "life" got in the way
But what was in my life
Inimical to Greece?

Those who put me off by their irony
Are unlike the Acropolis.
Or at least unlike the way it seems.
If the whole Acropolis were ironic,
I mean an ironic comment,

It would be a huge joke
Enjoyable frightening and laughable-at without end!

Go to look at it at sunset when it's PINK
My guidebook said. Good advice about anything, I suppose.
Or, after some road has been mended, when it smells like tar.
"When you are in love, go hear your beating heart."

Aeschylus and Socrates
Used to sit and chat up here
On the old rocks beneath the light of the very old sun
And one of their frequent subjects was
How young or old they felt or were.
"I am getting on, Socrates," says Aeschylus.
"Oh no," cries Socrates, "you still look like a boy!"

Plato would walk up here when he was tired
And talk to the alas-dead Socrates—
"Master I have come to a wall
And with statues and columns beyond it. What should I do?"
"Keep walking," the dead one counsels,
"And walking and walking, until the end.
You know it, know what to do—you are my best pupil."

What a car would do on the Acropolis
I can't imagine. But a deer or a beaver could
Build a home here while the light turned red
And sank into the Aegean.

The "wave of the future"
Never waved over the Acropolis.
It was never in any sense prophetic
Or meant to be prophetic
Of what was to come.
As long as the original lasted
The present was the only time.

Acropolis, Acropole, Acropolexis,
Acro—high, outermost, ultimate, never taken, undivulged,
Single-hearted, far, furious, added to *Polis*, city
High-up city, but what a curious city you are
With more god-objects per second than people in the street!

Greek people who are used to it
Say, "Oh, up there!"
On the great wall
A thousand miles of moonlight
Wrote Li Ho.
The Acropolis you can see all at once—
The Parthenon its nose
The Erechtheum its mouth
The Propylaea (entrance stairs) its teeth.

You can't find a glass of water
On the Acropolis or in Notre Dame
Or on the Great Wall of China. No use trying! There just isn't one there!

There are also no comic books on the Acropolis.
Though there are some on the subject of the Acropolis.
I buy a few down below, on the city's streets,
HELLAS KOMIKS and E PARTONIKI.

The tyrant Pisistratus used it for a fortress
To boss the life-loving Athenians until five hundred twenty-seven B.C.
At which time there was only one temple up here, the Hecatompedon.
About face! Present
Arms! You're under arrest! You have nothing but Persian papers, no good
    up here!

On Mount Athos you could be a Persian
Or a Thessalian or a Macedonian but you couldn't be a woman—
The slightest evidence and off you go! No females allowed—
Not even a butterfly or a squirrel.

"I have a guest over at my house."
But it isn't Apollo
I'll bet
And is it Hermes Trismegistus by any chance?
Apollo FLAYED someone
For competing with him in music.
How horrible, cruel, and sadistic (it was Marsyas).

As for Diana the punishment for seeing her naked was losing your eyes
Your liver and your heart. You were a dead Achaean
Never again to walk by the Aegean.

Yet they say it would be better for us
If we had this kind of mythology of our own
Instead of Daniel Boone and Jimmy Carter—
I look up at the sky and I see a constellation
Of Jimmy Carter signing an antipollution bill
And of Hermes tearing the insides out of a bear!

And to deal with the horrible tangle inside me
I don't know which to choose. Lucky, we have both.

The giant Athena statue
Gave the Persians pause.
Persian Number One said
If they have a goddess as great as that—
And Persian Number Three said
You're right! We'd better go!
Fast! Persian Number Two
Applied for citizenship
To become an Athenian.

It rains on the Acropolis I don't get wet
I am an American
The rain is twenty-five hundred years ago.

No one lives on the Acropolis tonight but the Acropolis Rat.

Acropole! Out of the earth
Came your marble, out of the sea
Came your earth, out of the air
The gods and goddesses
Who have been with you since you were zero years old!

The Acropolis has a strong format:
Temple, temple, temple, you have it up to here!
Gorgeous sources of divine misinformation,
One after another, blather blather blather, idiocy of the sky.

"The Acropolis has been
Removed from serious contention
By the historical operation
Of di-ectomy: removal of the gods."
So says the report.
But who is writing it?

Zones

When you have enough time
You can do it again and again
And that is how you make a forest
With each one the same
In being different
From all the others. You
"Really want to get something done"
How many trees, then, do you include in the forest?
The day isn't over
And the night isn't over
On the contrary the day has just begun
With a hooting and whistles
And a lark's clerical swirl
A pristine hopscotch of the scattering woodland repeats.
This doesn't reveal anything obvious
But rather gives a discrete
Powerful complicated understanding. Nature,
Which gives us the forest, is it wide
Or narrow from an absolute point of view?
It won't fit into a wheelbarrow;
And neither will time—
It has too many zones, as in the forest
Each tree has its own
And is its own
Dawn, morning, noon, evening, night.

A Changing China

I won't come with you, she said, to your demonstration.
She was afraid of becoming too admiring of what I did.
Later I met her at the Friendship Store.
We ate a dozen dumplings made with dog.
The handbook has illustrations
Of different breeds.
Here a collie, proud and tall,
Here a scotty, fun and small,
And the German Shepherd so munificent,
The cocker spaniel so glad to greet.
Three nights at the Peace Hotel.
It was filled with peace.
Peace rambled through its walls
Its stairways were peaceful its bathrooms were peaceful,
Everything seemed peaceful in the Peace Hotel
Now replaced by a more modern one called Golden Dog,
Le chien d'or, er shaiku ai ny pan.
I've lost the name and address
Of a Chinese writer held in house detention
Which some other writers gave me.
It's illegal, it's dangerous
If they find I had it I may be done for
I am hidden in the bamboo.
Big Business
Is coming to China
But Business that changes the score
China can hardly catch its breath any more.
I wasn't arrested I found the piece of paper.
Outer lobby there is a display of glass insects.
A bird flying over Kunming
Where the Fahrenheit temperature averages sixty-five
In the air of this unjust time.
In each room here is a hogshead made of bar glass.
Overseas Chinese are sleeping in the basement
And the stone five hundred feet high is topped by a bell.
Forgave its attitude toward dogs

After all we eat lobsters
Come here my little pet
Ah! Thlunk! The lobster is dead.
He lies in the Huang Po river basin with a stone for a head.
"No firecrackers in the chamber" the sign in each room.

Day and Night in Kuala Lumpur

The Malays, who are in the majority, are Muslims.
The Chinese, who have a lot of the money
To be found in the country, are Buddhists, twelve percent
Of the population is Indian, and they are Hindus.
The Muslims have a giant mosque
In the middle of Kuala Lumpur surrounded by cloverleaf-highway-type
    curve-offs,
A big line of bathrooms, for "cleansing" and
A number of minarets. The Chinese, Buddhist
Temples have music and smoke, and a great number
Of Buddhas because the more Buddhas there are the better will be
One's good fortune. The way some poets have a great many poems,
Collectors a great number of paintings, actors a great many roles
Or as a person may quite simply wish for a great many lovers or friends.
The Muslims, that is the Malays, rule the state. And the teaching
In high schools is in Behasa Malayu and you hardly have a chance
To get a state job if you are not a Malay, a Muslim.
One is born into one's religion here as into one's skin,
As into a tour group one can never forsake.
The Malay Sultans are exempt from laws,
They thrive in cool palaces. One sultan just cut off his gardener's head
With a sword because he displeased him in some way and legally nothing
    can be done. In K.L.
Gigantic high-rises shoot up everywhere
Full of offices and computers and Malay folk
Doing the financial work of Europe, America, and Japan. And if one longs
    for the village
(The panang), as the guidebooks say all Malaysians do ("they are essentially
    a forest and riverside people")
One goes there on the weekends. And in the soft arms of someone one goes
    to sleep.

In the Hindu park outside K.L. the monkeys
Are abundant and have quite a time! They line the great big stairways
That go up to the Holy Caves and they try to steal things from anyone who
    climbs up them. Often they succeed.

From me they get a Kleenex and from Karen nothing but she had nothing
Protrusive that they could get their hands on.
These monkeys' hands are essentially all fingers with no unnecessary part,
The fingers almost all bone.
They (monkeys) give to Kuala Lumpur its closest equivalent to Disneyland
But they are alive and have religious significance.
Anyone, any dead person, that is, might now be a monkey, which may be
    the reason
These monkeys are protected. It is as if Christians
Had Damned Souls and Saved Ones running along the stairs
Of their cathedrals and churches! However, one doesn't want to stay
Among these animals for long. Now, attired in batik,
Some persons go out, but many, many stay in, because it is so hot—
Although there is a big stuffed Santa Claus in a Chinese novelty store
    downtown.
Malaysia has had its life cycle interrupted. Universal modern technology
    has butted
Its nose arms and shoulders into the front window of the car.
What to do about it? So much has happened. So much has been suffered.
    So much has sweated, swatted, and wept. In batik then they go out
In the polluted hydrogen, oxygen, nitrogen, and all—And the Americans
    are here in their shirts
And the Japanese and the Germans in their shirts
And the French and the Italians in their sleeves
And the British who used to run the whole show
And built the railway station, for example,
Strictly according to Empire specifications:
It has a slanting roof capable of withstanding a large accumulation of snow
Snow that has never fallen in the Malay Peninsula. But now the British (as
    rulers) have gone
Taking their social classes and cricket games with them.
Their "club" remains, but it's no competition for the mosque
Any more, or even for the monkeys. You see a green lawn,
A white building, and that's it.
Malaysia, lying next to Thailand, has a sad reputation
For its atmosphere and for the non-jollity of its people.

The Thais are happier. As soon as you cross the border you can see it.
Even the pollution in Bangkok seems friendly
Compared to the pollution in K.L.; yet both are killers. Malaysia's poet
    laureate
Has a long white beard. He is writing a poem
About the contrasts of the high-rises and the villages,
In three-faithed Kuala Lumpur of the beautiful name.

Proverb

Les morts vont vite, the dead go fast, the next day absent!
Et les vivants sont dingues, the living are haywire.
Except for a few who grieve, life rapidly readjusts itself
The milliner trims the hat not thinking of the departed
The horse sweats and throws his stubborn rider to the earth
Uncaring if he has killed him or not
The thrown man rises. But now he knows that he is not going,
Not going fast, though he was close to having been gone.
The day after Caesar's death, there was a new, bustling Rome
The moment after the racehorse's death, a new one is sought for the stable
The second after a moth's death there are one or two hundred other moths
The month after Einstein's death the earth is inundated with new theories
Biographies are written to cover up the speed with which we go:
No more presence in the bedroom or waiting in the hall
Greeting to say hello with mixed emotions. The dead go quickly
Not knowing why they go or where they go. To die is human,
To come back divine. Roosevelt gives way to Truman
Suddenly in the empty White House a brave new voice resounds
And the wheelchaired captain has crossed the great divide.
Faster than memories, faster than old mythologies, faster than the speediest
    train.
Alexander of Macedon, on time!
Prudhomme on time, Gorbachev on time, the beloved and the lover on
    time!
Les morts vont vite. We living stand at the gate
And life goes on.

At Extremes

I had a dream about a polar bear
He seemed to want to inform me about something.
I have had a psychoanalyst but I have never had a soothsayer.
Even if my soothsayer were a polar bear I would not believe her (or him).
The men I see giving speeches in the public square know nothing at all
About anything I care about except how to move crowds
They like to move crowds the way Shelley wanted the West Wind to move
    his product.
Each might go and live with Janice in Florence in nineteen fifty-four.
Each might wake up some early spring morning oddly wishing to eat a
    piece of hard candy.
A former student of mine is doing very well, I hear, but his chronic anxiety
Makes him dissatisfied and unhappy, fearful that people don't appreciate
    him.
Well, some people appreciate him but he isn't satisfied with that.
He is sufficiently intelligent and ambitious but he gets headaches.
He will not go to Florence to live with Janice in 1954.
I am the only person in the whole history of the world ever to have done
    that.
No one knows when he or she is going to die. The polar bear probably
    never thinks about it.
He is wholly committed to life, unlike my former student,
Unlike Janice, unlike me. We are all committed to the life product.
What power is there in having done something once and then knowing
    automatically that it is for all time!
One, wearing a bathing costume of white featuring red dots, politely
    smiles,
If you don't try to come on to me I will show you the cliff
At which dolphins jump, but I couldn't promise
I used to say you don't need the sun when you travel first class
We were living in Greece unswayed by politicians
But we could be mightily moved by changes in the economy
Janice said to me one very hot summer day look at my feet
I said they're nice She said I didn't mean that, you silly
I mean look at all the tar on them from being on this beach
At that time there were no houses close to the sea.

You have to go back to your house.
You sleep there. Hotels are invented.
A hotel is where when you go there they have to let you in
If a room is available and you can convince them you can pay.
Michelangelo leaves Florence. He is just a man.
Ruskin and Michelangelo face each other across an oaken table.
When you are free it is hard to decide what is best.
There are no rooms in the hotel.
But now there is one. It hasn't been swept recently.
There is dust on the floor.
Gratefully, Michelangelo Antonioni sinks into a deep slumber.
Four of his great films are already made and another one is to follow.
The sheep were the best men at the sheepflies' wedding.
A noun perturbs an adjective with its slightly superior social class.
I'm the thing itself, the noun says.
Stay in love said Michelangelo and Antonioni woke up. Being bareheaded
    was serious business
In an arctic wind.
We were in good physical condition and not depressed.
We were fifty percent men and fifty percent women
We were afraid that half of us might be squid.
The nouns, wishing to be pampered, call the adjectives back
But it is the verbs, here by this thundering surf, that are triumphant.
Octopus come bearing blue-hatted children on their backs.
In a hotel you may sometimes find geniuses around
Probably they won't speak to you unless they need company.
Children clamber up to the roof of the hotel
Silently one of them wishes he or she were an octopus
Then one would be one's own village maybe one's own city
How could I have need, a child thinks, for anyone then?
The bird flies over the gray, deserted porch of the hotel.
I am the only one who saw Miss X at four-fifteen in the afternoon on
    June 2nd for the first time while attempting in a slight fit of nervousness
    to light up a Camel.
You are difficult to smuggle through customs.
Gypsy romance makes its appearance.

Everyone was fairly well satisfied—or almost—with someone else,

Even the ones who listen to the speakers and the one who walks around the city with his hands behind his back.

In Vinalhaven the old-timer's baseball game proceeds—

For some people, "reality" is represented by a prostitute, just plain business. Get down to facts.

The facts are that when you are fourteen or fifteen you want sex.

In some way or another you are going to get it.

By what process this turns into something with dominion over your life is unknown.

Theories abound. Small-town railroad stations. Bus stops. Inventions to replace teeth by glass.

Winter is ignorance. She picks the rose apart, trembling, with life in her fingers.

The polar bear swims toward the dam. He is part of a continuum.

POSSIBLE
WORLD

Peach Peach Peach

Tarzam

MONDO HUMP

Black   Kenneth

MONDO HAMPER

Reach Reach Reach   reach, reach

                    Don't you know

Sentence

                    along the beach

                    MONDO SEVERANCE

Mondo Universal Collectivity
Mondo aggrandizement
Mondo nothing left to teach

                              MONDO SENTENCE

        plague
                                                        trunk
                sunned
TAKE

                                        MONDO RESUMP-
                                                tion

        WIRY, VALLEY, CABLE, AIRY

                MONDO Completes

                    BUMP

MONDO OF CARRY
MONDO OF TEACH
                    the sun

            MONDO IS SUNBURNED DAIRY

Kenneth fled because of sacred thinking

            Mondo of unfloored beach

Scared he is walking
Unprepared he is walking
            UN
                    KNOWING

                    that ALL

                                            answers
                                        are within
                                            his reach
                    They are in

                            his STOMACH
        they are in his eyes and thoughts

            WILL power   beds
                        poison ivy

            A street of balls a horse of sounds a dachshund of
                                    breathing sighs
                    BABBLING
                            Those Wonderful WOMEN
Dog-hooked   SOUNDS
                    Ever to be Seen,
                            Embraced AGAIN
        How?
                                    Cause event effect

MONDO

back
            the
    in   basement
            Meantime

                                        AGREEABLY

        singing

    seaside BUMP

                MONDO

        MONDO SIMMER
                        MONDO GLASS

    "You can't beat that you just can't compete with that," said
                holding out to catch

                                        WHAT?

MONDO Hamper   Gallery,
          Cannery

                                        MONDO Slump

In a bright summer air a curious mondo

                              gravithump
          Haste!

     A bear, a trump
               genius
     the letters of the world
                         Mondo extreme

          Crying Hump

     crying personal seaboard faces

          aqua log
                    aqua log series thump

                                        Mondo Hump

     Invites   gladness   alights   madness
                    Mondo
Desert fastness
                    Mondo
                              invites fastness
                                        Mondo

          Serene

VOX

Vox when we are living together

POP

VOX POP

Pop when we are living together vox
opposed to capital punishment
slavery of fruit trees

Poppop the voices of the people   when we looked out
                                                                           banister
Vox let the people have a voice   over
                          saying

VOX   POP

we used to live there, all three
of that, mixed Kenneth
In whose dark dentyne shop
Liberty Bell for panters
VOX POP
Living well for theatres of three
                          VOX entertainment

and lively winter west
                                                       pop
          Pop
                          Pop
                                   Pop   Pop
                                                       pop

BLACK BOARD MONDO

                all aboard

     Mondo Peach

        flowering

     VAGUE and BUMP
                        hummingbird

     mondo some
You were wearing your see-through Adam-and-Eve fox costume

            I watched the labels come
                Remove the dome

            Abelard and Eloïse   1968 to nineteen ninety-one

            Astrid and Helicon
                                Mondo

            whatever
                    nineteen eighty
                But You

            Mondo SUNK
                and influence
        Affluence MONDO
                            mondo Scum
                                            on pond
            in nineteen eighty-two I find you

MONDO

summers   cocktail trees

Avenidas in which by shortcut brain dense populace

EVENING THOUGHTS

dense popular mondo

FOOL

To have been so brainless ivy cat fool

Iridium fool

Shot fool

Claxon seam tennis

Summer Hearts

MONDO

SHE

said   why NOT

explain

I can   but not

Why

Won't   her

We used to go there

raising great hotels

ONCE

WE   WALKED

all

over

PAR is

LOOKING FOR A BUMP

Arabian foot-chase

I plodded out a fire
in a vacant lot

MONGREL

Mongrels is unhappy

BLISTERS TRACE

extreme Himalaya park

MONDO

to
voting   sleep apart   BOMB

At this moment
SHE

Boisterous rovers
To other civic entities than ours
Have tendency to revitalize
Ancient and tricky orders
Of fan-tailed architectures
To surmise
That these are somehow better than ours
Is, as they say, to "wick the general"
As it is to "non-inflate the bed"
A bird harbors
That stone's distaste
For being what it was stopped by
Being bad.

Holes in the city walls

SUFFERING

BLACK
      GREEN
           RED
              WHITE
                    ORANGE
                          MIDDLE
                                SUN

apparently in tails
apparently in jeans
apparently in sober attire
apparently glad, and in good health

                          ALL THE PEOPLE
        ALL THE PEOPLE

            who have wanted things spread out

                    And they say

   "I don't do that kind of

        work"

Blue baby baboon helmets on holiday

      Go under the deck

      "I don't know"

POEMS BY GRASS BREASTS

MONDO

Finally you can do anything except not   DIE

EVEN   be at rest

BENEATH

HOPPO

Mondo Breath

Grace

Celestial mondo

This is the reason you wore

She wore

Waited

A Possible World

To a Bug

Insect on high
Now as on propeller plane
Down
To this glass's rim.
My wife's
Here and my friend Jean
Claude Vignes

                        I must
                        Swat you
                        Away

I wrote an opera libretto
In this Paris "apartment"
It's awfully small
To be called an apartment
Bug
You who from on high
Swoop down
May find it a department

                        Very big
                        A part of France
                        Or the bald heads
                        Of a university
                        Of silence
                        Where they allow
                        No (such) flies!

But the air is bigger
Go away
Oh no, now
Jean Claude
Wants to
See you

Janice
Does too. She says
"Kenneth, stop! wait!
It's an
Unusual housefly
One actually
Very rare in our day!"

"Oh!"
Jean Claude
Says. (And I
Considered you
Just a fly! Here

Have a piece
Of our
Cake)
Janice says
No, not
That. Instead

She brushes
You away
Then you're
Out

The window
No
More in our
Flat we
Can
Eat lunch
At last she
Says a
Very
Interesting bug

I've

Seen one in

A Vermeer

Says

A Ter Borch

The one

Children in it

In red

Janice said

Where now

Fly?

Not on!

Jean Claude

Or is it

You know

With the five

Dressed

"Oh!"

"Ah!"

Will you

Variations at Home and Abroad

It takes a lot of a person's life
To be French, or English, or American
Or Italian. And to be at any age. To live at any certain time.
The Polish-born resident of Manhattan is not merely a representative of
general humanity
And neither is this Sicilian fisherman stringing his bait
Or to be any gender, born where or when
Betty holding a big plate
Karen crossing her post–World War Two legs
And smiling across the table
These three Italian boys age about twenty gesturing and talking
And laughing after they get off the train
Seem fifty percent Italian and the rest percent just plain
Human race.
O mystery of growing up! O history of going to school!
O lovers O enchantments!

The subject is not over because the photograph is over.
The photographer sits down. Murnau makes the movie.
Everything is a little bit off, but has a nationality.
The oysters won't help the refugees off the boats,
Only other human creatures will. The phone rings and the Albanian
nationalist sits down.
When he gets up he hasn't become a Russian émigré or a German circus
clown
A woman is carrying a basket—a beautiful sight! She is in and of
Madagascar.
The uniformed Malay policeman sniffs the beer barrel that the brothers of
Ludwig are bringing close to him.
All humanity likes to get drunk! Are differences then all on the surface?
But even every surface gets hot
In the sun. It may be that the surface is where we are all alike!
But man and woman show that this isn't true.
We will get by, though. The train is puffing at the station
But the station isn't puffing at the train. This difference allows for a sense
of community

As when people feel really glad to have cats and dogs
And some even a few mice in the chimney. We are not alone
In the universe, and the diversity causes comfort as well as difficulty.
To be Italian takes at least half the day. To be Chinese seven-eighths of it.
Only at evening when Chang Ho, repast over, sits down to smoke
Is he exclusively human, in the way the train is exclusively itself when it is
    in motion
But that's to say it wrongly. His being human is also his being seven-eighths
    Chinese.
Falling in love one may get, say, twenty percent back
Toward universality, though that is probably all. Then when love's gone
One's Nigerianness increases, or one's quality of being of Nepal.
An American may start out wishing
To be everybody or that everybody were the same
Which makes him or her at least eighty percent American. Dixit Charles
    Peguy, circa 1912,
"The good Lord created the French so that certain aspects of His creation
Wouldn't go unnoticed." Like the taste of wheat, sirrah! Or the Japanese.
So that someplace on earth there would be people who were
Writing haiku. But think of the human body with its arms
Its nose, its eyes, its brain often subject to alarms
Think how much energy, work, and time have gone into it,
To give us such a variegated kind of humanity!
It takes fifteen seconds this morning to be a man,
Twenty to be an old one, four to be an American,
Two to be a college graduate and four or five hours to write.
And what's more, I love you! half of every hour for weeks or months for
    this;
Nine hundred seconds to be an admirer of Italian Renaissance painting,
Sixteen hours to be someone awake.
One is recognizably American, male, and of a certain generation. Nothing
    takes these markers away.

Even if I live in Indonesia as a native in a hut, someone coming through
    there
Will certainly gasp and say Why you're an American!
My optimism, my openness, my lack of a sense of history,
My distinctive facial muscles ready to look angry or sad or sympathetic
In a moment and not quite know where to go from there;
My assuming that anything is possible, my deep sense of superiority
And inferiority at the same time; my lack of culture,
Except for the bookish kind; my way of acting with the dog, come here
    Spotty! God damn!
All these and hundreds more declare me to be what I am.
It's burdensome but also inevitable. I think so.
Expatriates have had some success with the plastic surgery
Of absence and departure. But it is never absolute. And then they must bear
    the new identity as well.

Irish or Russian, the individuality in them is often mistaken for nationality.
The Russian finding a soul in the army officer, the Irishman finding in him
    someone with whom he can drink.
Consider the Volga boatman? One can only guess
But probably about ninety percent Russian, eighty percent man, and thirty
    percent boatman, Russian, man, and boatman,
A good person for the job, a Russian man of the river.
This dog is two-fifths wolf and less than one-thousandth a husband or
    father.
Dogs resist nationality by being breeds. This one is simply Alsatian.
Though he may father forth a puppy
Who seems totally something else if for example he (the Alsatian) is attracted
To a poodle with powerful DNA. The puppy runs up to the Italian boys
    who smile
Thinking it would be fun to take it to Taormina
Where they work in the hotel and to teach it tricks.
A Frenchwoman marvels at this scene.
The woman bends down to the dog and speaks to it in French.
This is hopeful and funny. To the dog all human languages are a perfumed
    fog.

He wags and rises on his back legs. One Italian boy praises him, "Bravo!
    canino!"
Underneath there is the rumble of the metro train. The boy looks at the
    woman.
Life offers them these entangling moments as—who?—on a bicycle goes
    past.
It is a Congolese with the savannah on his shoulders
And the sky in his heart, but his words as he passes are in French—
"Bonjour, m'sieu dames," and goes speeding off with his identity,
His Congolese, millennial selfhood unchanging and changing place.

Flight

The rocketship was waiting. I had to get on it.
It flew me away from the gardens,
It flew me away from the lake, the deliberate Como,
It flew me away from the strolls in the sun.
It didn't go very far but merely brought me
To a place where a few years previous
I had sat down writing some letters.
The rocketship hardly needed
Its rocket parts to do this, an ordinary plane would have done.
It took me to Hydra fifty years ago
If it didn't need rockets now, it needed them then.
I had no idea where I was going
The rockets made it sure I landed there
The island surrounded and supported by rocks
There were Norris and the waterside restaurant Msieu Oui-Oui's,
There were Dion and the ants in the courtyard
There was a large church bell and no water
(No wells) till the water boat came with its hose
There was Margaret there was Margaret's face
No opera and no concert
But lofty conversation, white bricks
A wall-hanging of *The Return of Odysseus*
No cars and no lawyer and no doctor
And the rocketship waiting again.

A Big Clown-Face-Shaped Cloud

You just went by
With no one to see you, practically.
You were in good shape, for a cloud,
With perhaps several minutes more to exist
You were speaking, or seemed to be,
Mouth open wide, talking, to a
Belted angel-shaped cloud that was riding ahead.

Roma non basta una vita

Kate, to Mario. You seem so happy. How can that be, when you've told me
  how depressed you are?
Responds Mario: I am so sad that I have come out on the other side. Ha ha.
On this other side spring flowers are visible,
Daisies and morning glory and poppies, a million poppies.
People smoke these in order to have veesions,
Mario says. Kate, then, Yes, I know, tell me.
M: You have to pass a church examination before you become an airmeet
  (hermit).
They recently have an airmeet who is crazy, perhaps from being on this
  drug
But maybe not. In any case he is crazy. He is appearing on the television
To tell of his psychawtic adventures so they are banning this theeng
That anyone, even a crazy one, should become an airmeet.
Mario: drives at eighty miles an hour. All passengers: experience fear. Kate:
Mario, stop! We aren't really on the other side! We're still in ordinary
  reality
And we don't want to die. Mario says I must have been dronk on the
  pawpie. I am sorry. I go slowly now.
Returning from the other side, he is sad again, but we get back.

The priest comes to bless the apartment.
There is magic in the air.
If we don't we may have bad luck.
The church could set fire
Or send out hooligans to wreck our sweet apartment.
No they wouldn't do that.
Meanwhile he is blessing.
He has already blessed the table at which you sit
Thinking of world history and of where we may go
Tonight. And now he is blessing the bed
I swear he is and now he passes out of sight

To bless the garlic on the terrace. He's right
To bless the windows
It's through them the poetry comes in
Blessing with fresh air the day and night
The priest is all set to go now
After the kitchen bless you and goodbye
A small token Grazie and may the Lord give you peace
I love this apartment. So, I think, do you. It's just right
For a blessing
On this contemporary, laid-back day.

3

Nothing is more striking than an airport
When, on a sparkling summer's noon,
You suddenly realize
That if the physician smokes beware
Of an updraught hitting you in the eye.
The airport is as beautiful as a plank
Thrust out over the water so you can see
Where you are going to, if not destined to, dive
You'll also see
Not a reflection of the world you leave behind
That has so violently to be reconsidered.

4

To see Rome's buildings and its history
I walked through the whole city and its streets
Unbothered by the traffic and the cars.
I said, lost in self-consciousness and thoughts
For Rome one life and span are not sufficient
To take its ancientness and forums in
One needs more than one's time and one's existence
To know the great piazzas and the fountains.
This promenade and leisure I'll remember

As part of something else, quiet and thinking,
Not let the future blur what comes to pass.
Saying which, I closed up the day and book
Of what there was, that spring and afternoon.

5

Here I am waiting for Mario in the gran caffé
On the Piazza del Popolo he is forty minutes late.
Arriving hand outstretched from his little car he says
I am sorry to be so late but it took much
Longer than I have expected. So many of the streets are forbeeden—his
    religious view
Of the traffic plan of Rome.

Sitting down, he tells me of his imaginary girlfriend (fidanzata)
A Spanish girl he invented and corresponded with
After a trip to Spain when he was in his twenties.
He in fact didn't have a fidanzata and, embarrassed about this lack,
Invented Paloma, to impress his friends. The correspondence he said
Was quite romantic and very hot and he enjoyed the letters
He wrote and those he received, on different stationery.
Where is Paloma now? Huh hah, I don't know he says. Maybe still in
    Spain, maybe not.

6

Better one day as a lion
Than one hundred years as a mouse.
Mussolini's theory
Which gives rise to doubts.
After this one day
You would be a dead lion
Or a live mouse
It would be the same thing.

Who is not part mouse
Except when Love is at the throttle
Or when we have drunk from the bottle
To a nice excess.
Or when a lion stirs in us at injustice
Unfairness, criminality, the pitiable
Then we may band together
And fight that as citizens.
Is Blake in agreement
With the ill-starred Benito?
No, Blake was in the private sector
And had no gangs of ruffians
Vulgar and full of hate. His lions
Were tigers of magnificence
Not rowdies for the fascist state.
Better one day as a giraffe
Than fifteen as an aardvark
May be easier to action,
Is harder to understand.

7

Francesco says to Jeanne (in French)
It was a lovely evening. Of course you did invite two people who represent
    to me
All that I find most disgusting and appalling in Rome, and are the reasons I
    have left it.
These were two Roman aristocrats Francesco detested. Aside from that
(A part ça) everything was perfect. Much laughter (though not by Jeanne,
And barely by Marcello, but after a while, some) followed by a delighted
    discussion
Of the phrase *"A part ça"*, which seemed to refute if only slightly
What another friend said about why Italians didn't buy his novels,
"There is no irony in this country, none at all!" At least, I thought so.

8

In Rome where I was often lonely
Romans when they have met you and think they may, just may, like you
If you're so forward as to suggest you might meet some time
For lunch or for a drink, characteristically say
Si. Ci telefoniamo, or ci sentiamo, which means
Yes. We shall telephone each other. Which means
That if nothing even a shade more appealing should turn up
If I haven't lost your number and if I remember who you are
I may phone you; but, when that happens, it doesn't mean
You two will meet, but only that a ci-telefoniamo again
Will swing through your chest like icicles
Giving you an impression that the real, true social life
Of actually being with Romans is about to begin.

9

Mario says (twelve years ago) that the end of communism is a great tragedy
For the intellect because now there is no place to turn
From the evils of capitalism.
He is waiting for something else.

10

Here you are in this miserable city in this wretched restaurant
Where you don't want to be at all (in fact we were in a mediocre outdoors
    restaurant in
The Campo de Fiori which wasn't such a bad
Place to sit though it was awfully hot, even at eleven at night).
You're here because of thees woman. Ah! I rejoiced, feeling suffering
But I have written about this conversation someplace else ("Talking to
    Patrizia," in One Train).
Patrizia said. So thees woman did she come back to you?
Are you then together now? No I said. Both our lives have changed.
    Patrizia says

I weel sand you my *Collected Poems*. You know when I start going through
     the papers
All over my apartment
I am finding some surprising good ones. Buona notte good night.
About a friend of hers who was supposed to meet us, Patrizia says E un
     ombra
She is a shadow you can never catch her!

                                    11

Alla Rampa, O restaurant
At which I sit with Jeanne and Marcello
And with Julian Beck and Judith Malina
On this late April night
When we have just come down from the Villa Borghese
Where one named Robert or (Jeanne) "Roberto"
Has given a concert on the piano
And where Marcello tells me
Of his strange life as a conductor
He knows he will be in Geneva in two years
For seven days and in Como in two thousand and five,
New York in September, et cetera
He has to live in the future with a hard hand on the past
(The scores of opera) and the present (not going mad)
And Julian and Judith tell me for the first time in thirteen years
Or thirty, I can't remember, they have their own apartment
They are doing a Living Theater stint in Rome
And for some reason they've been given, or found, an apartment
Can I imagine that, all those years without one's own place to live!
Yes I can imagine it and there is talk about the concerto
And then the evening comes to an end. I'm fifty three.
I look up at the beautiful night sky.

12

I used the wrong word
To explain the presence of Karen in my apartment
To Alessandra the cleaning woman,
Saying *la mia suocea* instead of *la mia cognata*
(My mother-in-law instead of my sister-in-law)
Ah, la bella giovane! Alessandra said
Or *E bella e giovane*, I didn't understand which
But knew as soon as I'd had time
To think it over, that I'd made a big mistake.
This kind of mistake I thought irreparable
Even though the apartment had been blessed.
The Father should have blessed my Italian vocabulary I said
To a window in a room where no one was present but me.

13

In San Pietro in Montorio
You can hardly stand up.
In the eternally flowing Tevere
You can't sit down.
In the Vatican you can eat cake
But you can't wear shorts.
Today you are turned away
From Saint Peter's and from coming before your God.

14

Mario comes over to the apartment
To put on his one-man show
About the Italian film magnate Dino di Laurentis.
Mario once worked for him
He seats himself behind a table
And puts on a Dino di Laurentis mask.
He presents di Laurentis as vile and corrupt.

Mario likes this kind of character
For his plays. Another of his one-man shows is Mussolini
Which has a considerable success.
To what extent do you think you, Mario,
Are like—Ha ha Mario says. Maybe you are right. I have been theenking of
   this.
Maybe you are right ha ha but maybe you are not.
It's true Mario that you always cut them down.
I try to, Mario says. The first play of his I'd seen
Years earlier was called *Felicità*.
Felicita is a beautiful girl who brings happiness
Everywhere she goes and as a result all is destroyed.
So then who is this one Mario says.

15

Rome is asleep. Finally.
But we are still up. Then, wildly,
The sound of a motor scooter. Rome
Isn't asleep. And we are up.

16

My daughter was born here and jokingly hoped
There would be a plaque
Commemorating this fact in front of the hospital
As there is in my heart.

17

Feathers, leathers above Roma it is all cardiography!
Chinese lanterns won't melt the snow (contemporary Russian poetry)
I am your vagabond and you are my faithful behind. Emerald tax!
   Seasons!
Whatever is below Rome is below the earth. Dynamites and traffic
   patterns.

No friend even knows I exist. Loneliness is my political party Veblen is my
    op-ed
Whose is the harp? Calendulas a-coming. Face of glitz.
But is it my own moaning that I hear? Never believe a dock rat. I am your
    peer.
Yes, I look into the objects. No, this contrariness is mine!
Time is absolved by it. Wreckers come on the scene. Self cognizance,
Self pity, all in one freaking sheaf. But I am of cosmogonies
As you are, bella Roma, of the days. Now both let's roll.

18

My new play Mario tells me which I have not yet wreeten
Is about an Italian who decides to becawm a Mooslim.
All of the Italian artists and intellectuals were communists
And when there is no more communism they do not know what to do
So they try the New Age, meesticeesm, pheesical feetness, Yoga, etc.,
But that dawsn't work. Then they deescawver the Mooslims.
They can be against capitalism again.

19

Dawn light not quite over the Victor Emmanuel Monument
But first late-night dawn streaks and we six standing there
The moon, the noon-gray light remembered not,
Or living in memory only. Ugly sledge-
Hammer effect of this pile of stones on the heart
And on the brain. Moving down toward the ruined deserted theater
Overwhelmed by the energies of creation
Could be anywhere (I suppose)
But happens to be here.
With what result? Blue. Rose.
So comes the dawn.

Paradiso

There is no way not to be excited
When what you have been disillusioned by raises its head
From its arms and seems to want to talk to you again.
You forget home and family
And set off on foot or in your automobile
And go to where you believe this form of reality
May dwell. Not finding it there, you refuse
Any further contact
Until you are back again trying to forget
The only thing that moved you (it seems) and gave what you forever will
    have
But in the form of a disillusion.
Yet often, looking toward the horizon
There—inimical to you?—is that something you have never found
And that, without those who came before you, you could never have
    imagined.
How could you have thought there was one person who could make you
Happy and that happiness was not the uneven
Phenomenon you have known it to be? Why do you keep believing in this
Reality so dependent on the time allowed it
That it has less to do with your exile from the age you are
Than from everything else life promised that you could do?

The Unfinished

A beautiful young woman with eyes like a leopard's
Walks past and
She does what a beautiful woman does. She indemnifies reality
From the stones and the Sundays to the hardest hit;
She makes malleable reality
So it will fit on a further beam. She unravels mutuality
So that it's tucked in a single seam. She is not Mrs. Bailey
My schoolteacher in the third grade,
Although of such truths poetry is made. I would not gladly
Live in a world without her, but that is fate.
She may be married to Tarzan. She may be Brendetta the Milk Maid.

The Moor Not Taken

Desdemona had her choice of numerous Moors.
But she chose Othello.
Why do I say "but"? Because Othello was a killer.
True, he had to be made jealous before he killed her
But how could anyone do that but a killer?
If we had been Desdemona, I am sure,
We should have chosen another Moor.
About five feet eleven, not Shakespeare's, another.
We get to talking and I ask him, finally, about the Moors
He says they don't really exist any more,
That the people of Morocco are no longer Moors
And do not recognize themselves in the person of Othello.
Your coffee was very good he said, and thanked me and went away,
Centuries too late to be taken, either by Shakespeare or by Desdemona.

Thor Not Taken

You have many good qualities, Ingrid said,
But I want my husband to be a Christian
And you still believe in the Norse gods, Thor the most outrageous.
I love you, love you, he said. But I cannot leave my gods.
Take me without Thor, he said. She quavered. Is that possible?
A child played with a set of wooden rabbits on the floor.
She remembered it fondly. The game set had been given to her by her
    grandfather, Bryggen-Thor.
Is that possible? she again said. The rabbits stayed the same while the girl
    grew up.
Now she was a woman. The cold wind blew against her ears.
Is it truly possible? she said. That I could have you—without Him?
Aye, merry, he said. And that day Christianity began its conquest of
    Norway,
Of sad Sweden, proud Denmark, and the Greenland isles.

Movement

Why did I take my life in my hands to see a few fish
And some gigantic cakes of ice
And to meet a few South American writers?
I could have imagined all this without coming here
And slightly increased my chances of staying alive.
I used to think it didn't matter how long I lived
But I didn't know how it did matter how much I saw
And could write about and how many people I met.
I'll have to take my life in my hands again now to go back
From life "down here"
I say "down here" because of the way it is on the map.
I have gone mainly east and south because that's where everything was that
    I wanted to see.
Finally, when I was almost sixty I went west, to China.
Where were things I wanted to see but I hadn't known
I could get to with my physical presence
Which is everything, the reason for life.

Primus Inter Pares

DAPHNIS AND CHLOE
To be the first ones there.

DOG ON THE DOCK
To be the first one there.

THE FACE IN THE SUN THE TASTE OF WHEAT
To be the first one there.

CANVAS
To be the first one there.

FORLORN LOVE, YOU IRREPLACEABLE COMMODITY, LET ME GO
To be the first one there.

PERSON IN A CLOUD
To be the first one there.

WE SPEND HALF A LIFE
To be the first one there.

AMALFI, TORN BY THUNDERSTORMS, IS WRECKED AND IS NO LONGER THE
  DESIRABLE RESORT IT ONCE WAS
To be the first one there.

THE LESSON COMEDY GAVE US
To be the first one there.

THE TRAIN STARTED UP BUT I WAS RELUCTANT
To be the first one there.

BYRON AS AN ACROBAT
To be the first one there.

SHOO FLY SHOO FLY AND OTHER GAMES AND ANOMALIES
To be the first one there.

ORDERLY CAFÉ

To be the first one there.

MUDDIED WATERS

To be the first one there.

JANUARY. EMISSARY. GOODNIGHTS

To be the first one there.

LATCHKEY

To be the first one there.

DECORATIONS REPEATED MANY TIMES

To be the first one there.

CLEMENCY

To be the first one there.

SHEEP FILLING ALL THE SPACE AROUND A HARBOR

To be the first one there.

Relations

La comtesse de Pierre, née de Mac-Mahon
Se promène sur le boulevard Mac-Mahon

H. J. M. LEVET, *Cartes Postales*

Julie, there was the time
You went on the *De Grasse* with E. E. Coulihan
Unknowing. He, a student, and you, met
One night, ship's ball, a party
For those not seasick. And you danced,
Oh how you danced!
And on deck afterwards, kisses
By the slippery dozens, and hands
Clutching the waist and back. Valery Larbaud
Admires Levet and goes to visit
His apartment rue Coulaincourt, the way R. Padgett
Three years back visits the provincial home of Reverdy
What different poets. For Levet
Fancy duds, white nights, a lot of women and a few poems.
For Reverdy a lot of poems and almost nothing else.
My grandfather
Gets dressed up in a blue serge suit, smiles.
He died (too)
He is a contemporary
Of Levet the first part of his days, of Reverdy the second.
Larbaud and he are exactly contemporary.
Coulihan dies young, age about forty.
You didn't forget him, and Coulihan didn't forget you.

Countess Julie, now, born a de Mac-Mahon,
Goes walking on the Boulevard Mac-Mahon,
The Arc de Triomphe visible
From where her family cemented its name.

Barking Dogs in the Snow

Barking dogs in the snow! Good weather is coming!
Good weather is coming to barking dogs in the snow.
A man changes only slowly. And winter is not yet past.
Bark, dogs, and fill the valleys
Of white with your awful laments.

A Memoir

This "dys-synchrony" one feels
>   In reading other people's memoirs
My life was not like that. But your life was
>   Your nationality and your "class"
Apparent in every sentence
>   If not in every word
So, I think, if I write mine
>   Everyone will know me
As the street runs past when it is well planned
>   Another street, to which it was the alley
But is now a confirmed street all its own
>   Frank O'Hara said to me
One thing that cannot be taken away from us
>   Is Panavision
The next year I went to Rome
>   When I read or even think of the memoir of the stone
It exhilarates, and deprives me
>   Of my own voice, the major word collection
Of mine in my own time
>   Greek columns rolled
As far as Selinunte
>   On the pastel fly
I could hardly include an erg of former energy
>   Without its being analyzed by myself
The clothes of all who walked past me
>   Contained other bodies than mine!
For they came one at a time
>   It is the study of languages
Of the polar bear heart
>   Weeks passed, I felt silly,
Useless, above all lonely, and apart
>   A heap of nothing
Rivers have names because there are few of them
>   Mud puddles generally none
Smell of the Tuileries
>   Glass hat racks attributing

What shall I put in my memoir
                Kansas City
Got off bus to get a haircut there
                Wearing a cowboy hat Kitty
You loved me with something to spare
                Opened to brightness
I thought I saw you down at the ship
                You did
I invented the airplane
                I said My gawsh! in a way
That people loved I walked Niagara Falls
                Hit my shoulder and you'll see
Gray's *Anatomy*
                Combining at a party
The boy the girl and the dog
                The old man
I hang in the air as if by accident
                Totally dependent on the social contract
And the good will of others
                And the evanescent spirit
I am here
                Love is there
Life is here
                Summer there
So no one's is a valid-to-ponder-about life
                Only the shallows
Of the green, at first, ocean,
                Then its purpler blues
I married into a family of indefinite objects
                When I was two years old
Indefinite stars above me
                Indefinite life my mother
Obscure relation to the sum
                Of all those people around me
Indefinite desk indefinite chair
                Vague flowers, vague tub, vague mirrors, pianos

I see my grandson, Jesse, now
          Marrying the same world.
The roof pays taxes
          Its tiles its taxes to the sun
I thought that love is
          A burning product
But now I see
          That it is random particles
One treatise about lunch is worth a thousand about hepatitis
          Until you have hepatitis
White is thrillingly indifferent
          To red, but blue is this rake
Secrets lost like forests
          Oh from what branch
Of tyrannosaurus have we fallen
          "In nineteen fifty-two I went left"
"In nineteen eighty-five
          I turned right"
I felt answerable
          To one purity and then to another
A bear cub
          Seen in Cincinnati
A tiger in Minneapolis
          I was sorry to have missed you
However without knowing about it
          You should never let your woman dance
With another man! the short guy—Indiano
          In Guatemala sometime in the seventies
An ocean trumping
          Its waves on the flush of the sand
Macho mysteries unavailable to me
          Lessons I learned later
Which are by then useless
          Seeing hearing Johnny Somebody
She was the best friend
          Of anyone who knew her

The blue tops
                Of the kitchen cabinets
The storm
                When it came we were both away
Who, as retro as a trumpet
                Leading a parade, is the other guy?
A film by René Clair
                Runs past me waving its arms
Times waiting in line at the Cinema
                Des Swans
In wit is pleasure
                Also in wind is pressure
Across the street is the
                Now across countries steal
O Italian girl in London
                Oh Italian girl
I hope you have
                Forgotten me
I give back what I have taken
                In return I want nothing
The birds walked over the
                Roof on which the dog is barking
Beeping to keep awake, cars coming
                With temperatures halcyon of increase
Different idols doing it
                The prize in the coffee
You can't get it out
                As known to myself when awake
And she said, Let's go away
                Engines on hillside to my right
Pomona on my left *en plein air*
                The doves in the tree Whingo!
Nineteen thirty-seven
                There is much less of me
Nineteen eight
                No existo

Nineteen eleven
                    Much the same
Nineteen ninety-seven
                    Bumps! Foghorns! Shepherds!
Owl attacks,
                    Supernumerary fogs and yet
Nineteen ninety-nine
                    Dawn Nineteen fifty-three
A song, Guy Béart tells me,
                    Needs to contain three things
Intellectual interest for the man
                    Sentimental interest for the woman
And fun for the child
                    A "sexist" idea
That year glorious summer came
                    On five spring evenings
Supernumerary lists
                    Lists for the young and the aged
I've seen old people standing in holes
                    That bulldozers left in the concrete
Others assailed by diamonds
                    Curiosity about anthills
How many stares at Greek
                    Without learning a word of it!
Apollo and Thespia
                    There was my life as a life
I thought without Greek I can't lead it
                    I think without Greek I have led something else
Of Italians there was Poliziano
                    One among many
Or several at the door
                    I bring home the book *Tutte le poesia italiane*
She cries (Janice)
                    "All of Italian poetry!"
Greedily we attack it but it
                    Is the complete poems

Only of Poliziano
                Chi non sa come e fatto el paradiso
Guardi Ipolita mia
                Negli occhi fiso
That's great Janice said I
                Said Yes isn't it great
We then won't have to nominate
                Any more heroes for our sensibilities tonight, we have Angelo
I once thought "Am I Angelo" I then thought
                "Angelo makes masterpiece
After masterpiece
                Alas I am not Angelo
I am reading work of Angelo
                Songs cease. Begin and cease."
On the desk in the chair and in bed
                Ipolita's eyes
Whose values seem ever to increase
                Until finally
Raymond Chandler and Poulenc take to the wall
                In superior agitation
Mickey Mouse and Rumi
                Take to the wall
And all of the Berber nation
                Grandma and clipboard stick to the wall
If you can get in this you can get out of it
                Type of reaction meanwhile raccoon
All sweetness is gone
                Meaning some sweetness (I have known so far)
Is gone
                You Hotel de Fleurus is gone
English grammar is gone
                As for French you "have to dream in it"
Try to make things cease
                Without even whispering
On a pillow that book lay lighting
                Up the whole bed Janice said stay in bed

It is worth clocking for
                    Then is all sweetness
I wondered if anyone would ever
                    Love things in the same way
Some did even many I wasn't the only one
                    A shower head an oyster
Catching it is enough
                    While—a bedroom window at their scene
I throw the bicycle up
                    In the air then catch it I am so young
Volatile evergreen
                    Keep walking sensations in shoulders
Plus throat You travel too much
                    M. Gallimard said to M de G
You flatter yourself too much
                    I spoke to myself
Her strangeness
                    His confusing ways
Her supposed militancy
                    His regret
Her natural poses
                    You want everything
As one
                    When we left it was the market still there?
This problem of Berkeley's
                    That is itself so unreal
Gravity goes to sleep so does plywood in the wall
                    Its tenure like a baby's is long
O life of the Piltdown
                    The High Renaissance
Somebody up there has done something!
                    M's sister comes down to the bar
I am humming with praise
                    We are under the covers
It is the time of the jazz age
                    That succeeded the other

Muggsy Spanier and Bunny Berrigan
                    I've flown around the world
In a plane
                    Discovering Communism
Karl Marx does the dishwork
                    Hegel lives on in memory
In any event the Marxists helped
                    The good people to escape
Later we would form an army
                    Beside some ludicrous pump
It created
                    I had (we had) to undiscover it again
Okay! Janice said let's
                    Read all of Poliziano
I found three poems
                    I might almost be able to read
"Chi non sa come"
                    And two others
The rest were too
                    Unpossessed by our vocabularies
Roland jumped up
                    From his intriguing chanson
We never spent much money
                    We were thoughtful and lost
Whereas Poliziano
                    Once he entered the diplomatic service
Angelo hello
                    I am plenty of these
Everyone is an envelope
                    Inside which one is hiding
Some trees
                    At last I am feeling in love
The murderous rise of the ship
                    Tormenting the created water
In any case once he did
                    Entered the service

At twenty-six
                Had so little time to write poems
That except for a few official occasions
                He stopped
But what would old Poliziano have written
                "I live under seven stars
As an eagle might
                Mais attenzione!"
Would this high-thinking-feeling Italian man
                Even recognize my presence in the street
Well I had others Janice and I drink tea
                So keep reading him ignorant
Intellectual (relatively) wandering
                Through a culture
Someone is singing
                On the landing below
The arc strike of a pen on paper
                Doesn't put one in the show
However much we try
                Like the moon I have tried to be everything
Except to be that
                Completely other impossible
Said the bite professor waddling
                Jane Henderson's clear stained rose
You are the substitute for that
                With no vultures it is raining
I wrote down Hawk I wrote
                Then hog I wrote then hock I wrote
You are the substitute for that!
                Don't get so excited,
Moving away from the Maison des grands clichés
                You'll spy a building on your right
You may find worth entering
                But don't go there yet it's your tomb!
The forsythia weathers the trip
                This rose (envelope)

Is bright
                This (rose) letter is breathing
I passed their schoolhouses wanted to teach
                Radiator central
Telling
                Dangerous friends everything
Needing no further work
                The friend who
Constantly reappeared
                In dreams, as I
Had wished him to be
                Though still a puzzle
He was, too, when alive
                But this time I knew
That he was dead and put back together
                I was always afraid
He would fall to pieces again
                And threw my dog in the air
May have hurt him when he fell down
                Fear resuscitated
He is himself again
                To walk out and see Jenna
In her white two-piece tumbling tutu
                We can graduate from college
Together I said and off we went
                To Yankee Stadium and the Bronx Zoo
Grace Paley walking past my apartment
                In a march against injustice
Lionel Abel philosophizing on a bar stool
                Jim Dine mangiatore dei sui colori (eating his paints)
Larry Rivers installing some pipes
                In a lower East Side apartment, waiting
A bus comes by containing
                The even-handed breeze
Maria Teresa Cini wobbling
                When the elevator comes to a sudden stop

And saying

        A poet should never see an apartment like this

John Ashbery gets tight

        Noel Chatelin smacks him

With a five hundred franc bill

        The Life of the Bee

M. says in Paris

        Probably your real life is here

Since you like it so much

        That it's almost unnatural

And N. said

        Here in Rome you will find the true life

Down around the stadium

        Waking and out looking at those old stones

I thought that maybe she was right

        The stone life one admires

A little and then a lot

        Then some sprinkling afternoon with sunshine not at all

Your real existence is with us your friends

        J. putting her jacket on backwards

Makes us laugh

        The great archway

With her necklace of brilliants

        Naked J.T.

Already done justice

        The real life maybe the real life

Is sex

        The hills are the main civilization

The old woman holds the pup

        Tightly in her fragile arms for it is snowing

Noon, luck, days on a planet

        Is the one room where lovers stand apart

I was once one of those

        As you keep laughing about at breakfast

How could you ever have been

        Town grapefruit town breakfast

I have to go back to Penn Central before daybreak
                    Train leaving at dawn
The smell of cold artillery and mixed up rifles
                    Gives way to several novels by Booth Tarkington
I came to a place where there were a lot of birds
                    Not alien forms
Oh well Past is past (James Schuyler)
                    Whereas the future
Do you dream about it much
                    I never think about the future
She says
                    Scratching a mirror of her dress
Catwalking the incumbency, matador
                    Here is thy sling
Aboveboard there is a tourniquet sliding
                    Halfway between some ditch dock doors
We are through playing there
                    The past is an energy without thought
All proposals about it are vipers
                    You take the first egress and I'll get lost
The banners
                    That told not of triumph
But of the opening of an audio equipment store
                    The ten lost driveways of Venice
Never to be thought of or stored
                    In memoria universalis
Recognition of the spring signs
                    The first note of the violin
Sappy happy hibiscus
                    The lanterns of lips and of tongue
I secretly or not so secretly wanted to sail
                    An orchestra island
Catastrophic tour
                    But instead lay insolvent
To play bingo
                    With a foreign correspondent

Your student grant money amounts to more
                Than here is paid to a bank president
How about some coffee
                Asked the rugs
Is Turkey that invisible?
                I wondered myself
Walking up the grass
                Highway a middle precedent
Wandering down this slope
                Hearing about hideaways to have been
The way Trollope wrote *Phineas Redux*
                And *The Eustace Diamonds* and Balzac wrote *Père Goriot*
Interest in blackmail
                Or sleeping on top of Harry's Bar
Loved Sciascia's *The Day of the Owl*
                The rhythms of fingers
Re-write Beethoven's Fifth Symphony
                Nor Mozart's hammerklavier quartet
Newton and Tito and Felix the Kat
                Heroes planned to protect disorder
What poor man is the champion
                Who denies old age?
Coincided we look around
                For the parallels that make good arches
A stadium more than a tree
                A compromise with Lorenzo the Magnificent
One day a kitten falls in a well
                And is rescued by Dionysius
Which is the full name of Dion
                Of Hydra age five
My daughter is a friend of his
                My memoir for a moment gets fat
And glows if impossible to write
                Walking around as if with gods in that garden
And demigods themselves were our persons
                For fifteen minutes it was light

The dogs of darkness carried in
                  Waking up I thought "I am forty"
But actually I was fifty
                  Paul Klee painting with delight
On a very small scale like a jitney
                  Feel memorially enclosed in the night
When we walked it together
                  The "ho-ha!" of walking
Beats the "who-ha" of sleeping
                  In the piranha tank
Said Leonard circa twentieth century
                  I want the moon to be my problem
All the time
                  Who would deny that
The circus said
                  I mean the varied voices of the circus
That I heard in Paris
                  Janice stringing out clothes on a line
And the cat, the poor cat
                  In the well-bottom
Not every man is fortunate enough
                  To visit Corinth
With its agora of up-for-sale beauties
                  The Greeks, worried, I remembered
Bones and muscles are not but almost enough
                  We'd also need divine hindsight
To be born then
                  Children's footprints on the marble
Pages stuck
                  In the machine
Of the unpainted square
                  Water turning into icicles
Woman being the scoreboard of man
                  Four wins and one baby
The showplace of stardom
                  Numbered, the Tigris and the Euphrates

Man being the showplace of woman
                    Castigated scored rebuked
And the best conversation of the time
                    When I'm awake am I available
Protons! my friend murmurs we have to go out
                    And get this down
Envy encamped against people
                    Bitterness encamped against people
Bees that made sense
                    To purpose in the sand
You lifted your head up
                    And I sat down at night
How do the Frenchies do it?
                    Said Rory circa nineteen seventy-eight
Ambusculating Paris
                    Right shadows on trees
Overcoats planned not by headlights
                    But coasts of butterflies
The sheep god damn this tavern
                    A rumor of foresight
After the drinks and news came out
                    Not Africa but could have been
I love that country
                    That country is not in sight
They do it by theories
                    Immaculate conceit
When I went to bed
                    O material objects
Stones made of sunlight
                    It would appear
Better
                    Maybe Ipolita
Outliving her golden age
                    Treachery was in the air
From best beloveds it was still there
                    Planked me into some residencies of my life

Okinawa hand grenades
                Columbia the tests
Fiery life as a patient of psychoanalysis
                My freebooting life as an expatriate
Pardon me will you open that door
                Time-mates of Pluto or of Theophrastus
I am busy don't bother me please
                Existence among friends as amidst idiots
Or hornets or pleasing angels
                Habituation to paying by the mule
A wayward assumption
                When Janice felt lost
It was easy but I had to find her
                She was also a supreme self
As was Katherine
                Who was in my arms
I felt Let us no longer take up arms
                One against the other
I thought for at least ten years afterwards
                I've wasted my life I didn't stay in Paris
In fact my life went ho ho ho
                And flattened itself out in New York
I could have made a memoir that was all loss
                Lost Marina lost marriage lost Paris lost inspiration
I would live in this Memoir for days
                But a birthday was obvious
Became all too clear
                I hadn't wasted my life because it wasn't wasted
My head was in my hands
                But I was only thirty-five
Never to slump again
                In quite that same fashion
Suddenly the universe is awake
                You used me up but I was a dog
In nineteen eighty-six
                Scared book ambitious for experience

Besides the laments that were wasted
           Came back and back and back
Inglorious afternoons
           Spent near the bump shack
A woman's favorite tune
           Sung next to me in the unCadillac
That joy of hand touching
           Grave genius
I felt always
           For two or three minutes a month
Did I thought "These will stay"
           Commanding?
There was plenty of time
           A man and woman lost in the jungle
Hardly wasting their time until they get out
           But she saying It is wasted
Wasting my time eating and drinking
           Because there is only one life
The memoir shows how not it
           Existence to promise is
No one can lead it
           Except by arriving too late
But then you have it
           And this palaver is foolish
One thing could make me happy
           Two things could make me glad
To have intelligence enough to find
           A third thing
And so forth
           Until I had
The billion elements gyrating from central
           Self
To make useful one third of a day
           And its ready existence in the soul
As defined by Mitsugo
           "Garden of flash seasons"

But we grow cold
                    Eating and drinking just to be waiting
For those millions of things to come
                    So give me five I'll
Be happy
                    Give me fourteen my mind be on a roll
One agora in a blue cashmere sweater
                    Three agoras (pl?) in white angora sweaters
Nineteen steam chimneys away
                    The board with a nail in it
Each is precious
                    Being of course evanescent
I don't give up
                    I take the boat
It is full of Carpaccios!
                    Seventy Saint Ursulas
The bargains are overflowing
                    The peach tree gets what it can
It gets blossoms and peaches
                    And the kindly stares of the populace
This "middle-aged" man is crying
                    The peach tree gets that too
So life is wasted from the beginning
                    There is no way to use enough life
Not by excess can you do it
                    Nor by sparely imagining
Maybe only by working your way through it
                    Like voltage or a rabbit
But the dream is that there is one
                    I think of the past woman to help move this one on
And destroy it with vivacity
                    Why do you wish to see more things
Act as if you were thirteen years old
                    Prepare to see Hamlet
Is superficial
                    I want to be a song

Tendency to walk over here city
                Now dormant or as they say asleep
While waiting with everybody else
                To see what comes
I regarded the malignancy as only fear
                It would have to be written about too
The memoir
                Is a raincoat
A seed
                A nothing
Saint Joan is not in it
                One fraction of humanity
Making a huge difference
                Imaginable to me at fifteen
Though not much later
                Photocopying machines and General de Gaulle
Are not in it
                In yours maybe but not in mine
Robert closes the door
                The steeplechase is beginning
This rope has the smell of the Regatta
                Ave opera
The elephant's foot
                There won't be much traffic
Janice said
                I said There isn't any
There was very little
                Torn was a suit
She had wanted to wear
                Waking up and walking though the streets
A far cry from Gene Kelly
                In *Les Demoiselles de Rochefort*
Dancing all around the harbor
                A pale sheep
The whiskey or the brandy
                The coke stand wouldn't take us in

It was very warm out even the stones
        Having no old-fashioned significance
This is prohibited by language
        Also by boys and girls in long shirttails
The sea cancels out the least resistance
        That wallet the breeze great medicine birth
Everywhere I look
        To sneak back on my experience
Life what an eroded stone you are
        And plant you with gasps of poetry
Now that I can face them directly
        These streets and these alleys not my own
When I went to the Rome opera
        That bent it
You have a beautiful head
        The young woman said
She was headed into a life of resentment
        And contentment
If I thought What do I know
        I started a memoir
What do I care
        If she imagines silence?
It won't work from over this way
        She has had a new baby
The memoir is five feet two
        But no longer
Enduring what we tell each other
        I am a fragment
Would you, lilac, put in a school
        Of this morning
Vanish from those
        Hot lips forever
That stake and seal your mortality
        And to whom would I be speaking
If all signs were you?
        Get only so far

Then the general trail of humanity
                Soon there's no more speaking
But have worked on whatever there was
                An honest face
Asking a quiet question
                In some culture at five a.m.
Or the cannon's boom
                The darkness seems more and more ridiculous
Vigorously on its way
                But not yet a fixed idea
This existence like another
                Taking place

A NOTE ON THE TYPE

This book was set in Janson, a typeface long thought to have been made by the Dutchman Anton Janson, who was a practicing type-founder in Leipzig during the years 1668–1687. However, it has been conclusively demonstrated that these types are actually the work of Nicholas Kis (1650–1702), a Hungarian, who most probably learned his trade from the master Dutch typefounder Dirk Voskens. The type is an excellent example of the influential and sturdy Dutch types that prevailed in England up to the time William Caslon (1692–1766) developed his own incomparable designs from them.

Composed by Creative Graphics,
Allentown, Pennsylvania

Printed and bound by United Book Press, Inc.
Baltimore, Maryland

Designed by Soonyoung Kwon

4/30/03

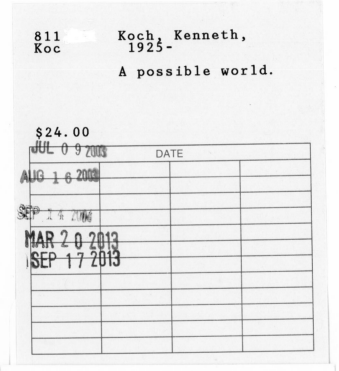

JUL 0 9 2003	DATE		
AUG 1 6 2003			
SEP 1 4 2004			
MAR 2 0 2013			
SEP 1 7 2013			